spot

PETS

FISH

by Mari Schuh

AMICUS | AMICUS INK

tank

mouth

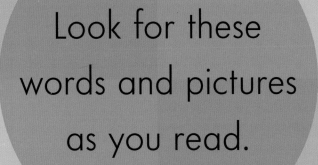

Look for these
words and pictures
as you read.

scales

fin

Look at all the fish!
How many fish do you see?

tank

Do you see the glass tank?
It has rocks and plants.
Fish hide there.

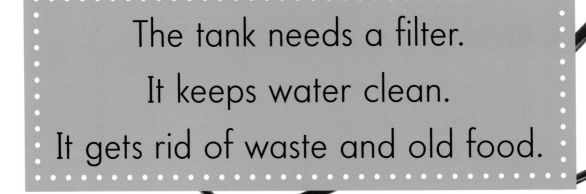

The tank needs a filter.
It keeps water clean.
It gets rid of waste and old food.

mouth

Do you see its mouth?

Fish eat tiny flakes.

They eat pellets.

Do you see its scales?
They are hard.
They cover a fish's soft body.

scales

fin

Do you see its tall fin?
It keeps the fish
from rolling over.

A goldfish swims around.
It nibbles on food.
It is a fun pet!

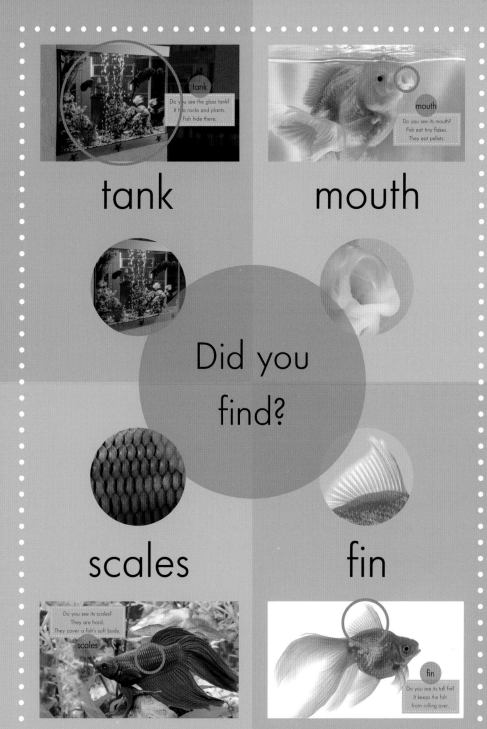

tank

mouth

Did you find?

scales

fin

Spot is published by Amicus and Amicus Ink
P.O. Box 1329, Mankato, MN 56002
www.amicuspublishing.us

Library of Congress Cataloging-in-Publication Data
Names: Schuh, Mari C., 1975- author.
Title: Fish / by Mari Schuh.
Description: Mankato, Minnesota : Amicus/Amicus Ink,
  [2019] | Series: Spot. Pets | Audience: K to grade 3.
Identifiers: LCCN 2017035034 (print) | LCCN 2017045498
  (ebook) | ISBN 9781681514499 (pdf) | ISBN
  9781681513676 (library bound) | ISBN 9781681522876
  (pbk.)
Subjects: LCSH: Aquarium fishes--Juvenile literature. |
  Fishes--Juvenile literature.
Classification: LCC SF457.25 (ebook) | LCC SF457.25 .S38
  2019 (print) | DDC 639.34--dc23
LC record available at https://lccn.loc.gov/2017035034

Printed in China

HC 10 9 8 7 6 5 4 3 2 1
PB 10 9 8 7 6 5 4 3 2 1

*To Alexa, Aubrin, Cage, Emma,
Kayden, and Westin at
Wakanda Elementary School —MS*

Wendy Dieker, editor
Deb Miner, series designer
Ciara Beitlich, book designer
Holly Young, photo researcher

Photos by Dreamstime 1; Getty 14-15;
iStock 3, 10-11; Shutterstock cover, 4-5,
6-7, 8-9, 12-13

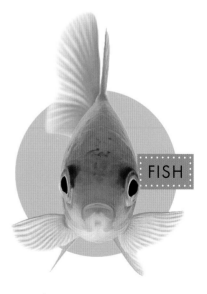

FISH